I0797713

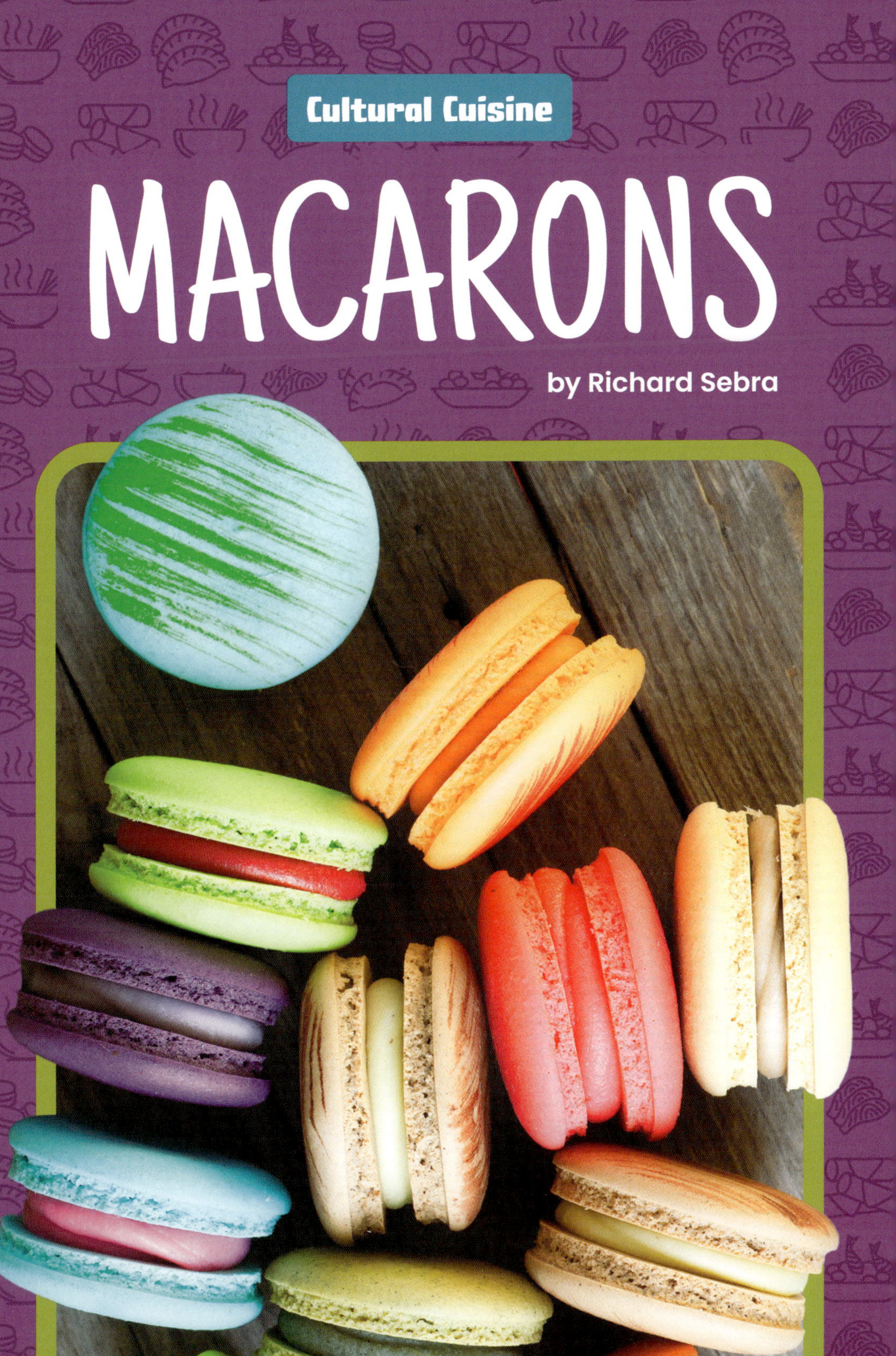
Cultural Cuisine
MACARONS
by Richard Sebra

abdobooks.com

Published by Pop!, a division of ABDO, PO Box 398166, Minneapolis, Minnesota 55439.

Printed in the United States of America, North Mankato, Minnesota.

082020
012021

THIS BOOK CONTAINS RECYCLED MATERIALS

Cover Photo: Shutterstock Images
Interior Photos: Shutterstock Images, 1, 9, 13, 19, 25; iStockphoto, 5, 6–7, 7, 8, 12, 14, 15, 17, 18, 20, 21, 22, 26, 27, 28, 29; Maurice Rougemeont/Gamma-Rapho/Getty Images, 11

Editor: Sophie Geister-Jones
Series Designers: Candice Keimig, Victoria Bates, and Laura Graphenteen

Library of Congress Control Number: 2019954988

Publisher's Cataloging-in-Publication Data

Names: Sebra, Richard, author.

Title: Macarons / by Richard Sebra

Description: Minneapolis, Minnesota : POP!, 2021 | Series: Cultural cuisine | Includes online resources and index.

Identifiers: ISBN 9781532167768 (lib. bdg.) | ISBN 9781532168864 (ebook)

Subjects: LCSH: French cooking--Juvenile literature. | Macarons--Juvenile literature. | Ethnic food--Juvenile literature. | International cooking--Juvenile literature. | Food--Social aspects--Juvenile literature.

Classification: DDC 641.5944--dc23

WELCOME TO DiscoverRoo!

Pop open this book and you'll find QR codes loaded with information, so you can learn even more!

Scan this code* and others like it while you read, or visit the website below to make this book pop!

popbooksonline.com/macarons

*Scanning QR codes requires a web-enabled smart device with a QR code reader app and a camera.

TABLE OF CONTENTS

A RAINBOW OF FLAVORS

People line up outside the **pastry** shop. The smell of sweet sugar fills the air. Inside the shop, a baker removes a tray of macarons from the oven. He lets the round cookies cool. Later, he will add a filling.

WATCH A VIDEO HERE!

Bakeries often display their macarons using tall stands.

When buying macarons, people choose the combination of flavors they want.

The baker's case holds macarons of many colors and flavors. The pink ones taste like raspberry. The yellow ones taste like lemon. There are chocolate and vanilla macarons too.

The macaron is one of France's most famous desserts. It consists of a delicious filling inside two **meringue** cookies.

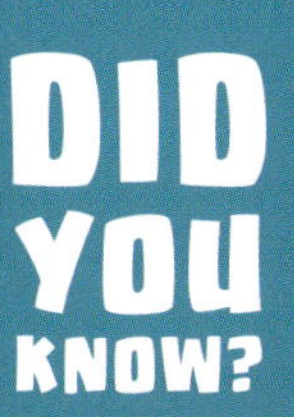

Macaron is pronounced mac-uh-RON. A macaroon is a completely different kind of cookie. It is made from coconut.

Coconut macaroons are often dipped in chocolate.

People practice making macarons to find the right baking time.

BAKED JUST RIGHT

Macarons are famously tricky to make. If the cookies are baked too long, they dry up. If they are underbaked, they become a gooey mess. But if baked just right, macarons are soft, tasty treats. It is no wonder they are loved all over the world.

CHAPTER 2

A ROYAL DESSERT

Today, macarons are known for their distinct look. But macarons started out as single cookies. The cookies were made with egg whites, almond flour, and sugar. They had no filling. And they came in just one flavor.

COMPLETE AN ACTIVITY HERE!

People still make macarons with the original almond flavor.

Catherine de' Medici brought this recipe to France in the 1500s. She was Italian. But she became queen of France. She brought **pastry** chefs with her to the country.

The small almond cookies became known as macarons de Nancy.

In the late 1700s, the **French Revolution** started. Two **nuns** fled to the town of Nancy. To earn money, they baked and sold macarons.

The **meringue** cookies quickly

became popular.

The nuns were known as Les Soeurs Macarons*, or "The Macaron Sisters." People can still visit their store.*

In the 1900s, double-decker macarons became the most common version.

In the 1930s, Pierre Desfontaines had an idea. He took two cookies and added a creamy filling. The result was a delicious cookie sandwich. He began selling the filled cookies at Ladurée, his **café** in Paris. Soon, bakers all over France were making this version.

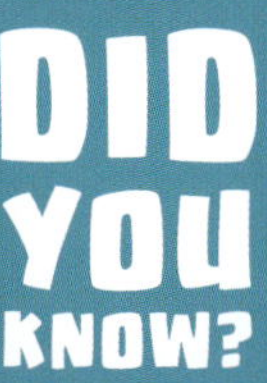

Ladurée now has locations all over the world. Its shops sell more than 15,000 macarons each day.

Ladurée has been selling pastries in Paris, France, since 1862.

CHAPTER 3

IN THE KITCHEN

Making macarons involves several steps. **Pastry** chefs make the cookies first. They mix almond flour and sugar in one bowl. In another bowl, the chefs beat egg whites until they are fluffy. Then they add vanilla and more sugar.

TRY A RECIPE HERE!

Chefs try to make all cookies in a batch exactly the same size.

Bakers tap pans on the counter before placing them in the oven. It removes air bubbles.

Next, chefs add the dry ingredients to the egg mixture. They stir to create a smooth **batter**. Then, they squeeze the batter onto the pan in little circles. When the pan is full, chefs let it rest for a while.

That way, the cookies will rise in the oven.

Macarons bake for about ten minutes.

DID YOU KNOW? **When macarons bake, they develop ruffles of air bubbles. These ruffles are called feet.**

The temperature of the oven affects how much the cookies will rise.

A macaron's filling is often the same color as the cookies.

Traditional macarons have a buttercream filling. Chefs mix butter, powdered sugar, milk, and vanilla together. They put filling on the flat side of a cookie. Then, they place another cookie on top.

Each macaron's appearance should be smooth and neat.

RECIPE CHECKLIST

COOKIE INGREDIENTS

- 3/4 cup almond flour
- 1 cup powdered sugar
- 2 egg whites
- 1/4 cup sugar
- 1/2 teaspoon vanilla

FILLING INGREDIENTS

- 1/4 cup unsalted butter
- 1 teaspoon milk
- 3/4 cup and 2 tablespoons powdered sugar
- 1/2 teaspoon vanilla

Makes 16 macarons

INSTRUCTIONS

Cookies:

1. Mix flour and powdered sugar in one bowl.
2. Mix eggs, vanilla, and sugar in another bowl.
3. Gently combine bowls and mix together.
4. Pour the batter into a pastry bag.
5. Squeeze small circles onto a baking sheet. Let them sit.
6. Bake for 10 to 12 minutes.

Filling:

7. Mix butter until creamy.
8. Add milk, sugar, and vanilla, and mix until light and fluffy.
9. Use a pastry bag to put the filling onto the flat side of a cookie.
10. Place another cookie on top.

CHAPTER 4

AROUND THE WORLD

Macarons can be found all over the world. They are especially common in France's capital city of Paris. Many bakeries make macarons. And some specialty shops sell only macarons.

LEARN MORE HERE!

Traditional macarons have soft, pastel colors.

Sometimes, particular shops are known for making specific flavors of macarons.

Macarons come in hundreds of flavors. Chocolate, almond, and raspberry are common flavors. But **pastry** chefs often put their own twists on the recipe. They try new colors and flavors. Chefs also use different fillings. Some macarons have jam in the center. Other versions hold lemon curd or **ganache**.

MACARON FILLINGS

Each kind of filling has its own texture and flavor. Lemon curd and jam are fruit-based fillings. Ganache and buttercream are smooth and creamy.

Because macarons are so hard to make, many people choose to buy them in shops.

At many shops, people choose which macarons they want. They can mix and match. The macarons are packed into a box. People sometimes give a box of macarons as a gift.

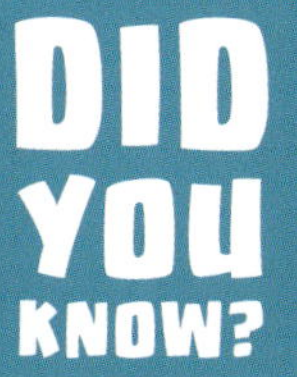

Macarons are everywhere in France. Even McDonald's sells them.

Boxes of macarons often have fancy decorations.

MAKING CONNECTIONS

TEXT-TO-SELF

Making macarons involves several steps. What is the most complicated food you have tried making?

TEXT-TO-TEXT

Have you read other books about desserts? How were those desserts similar to macarons?

TEXT-TO-WORLD

Chefs use many flavors for macaron cookies and fillings. How do you think they find which flavors taste good together?

GLOSSARY

batter — a mixture of flour, egg, and milk or water.

café — a restaurant that often sells baked goods.

French Revolution — a period of political and social change in France between 1789 and 1799.

ganache — a sweet, creamy chocolate mixture used for filling or frosting.

meringue — a type of delicate baked treat made with egg whites and sugar.

nun — a female member of a religious order.

pastry — a baked food item with a high fat content.

INDEX

ONLINE RESOURCES

popbooksonline.com

Scan this code* and others like it while you read, or visit the website below to make this book pop!

popbooksonline.com/macarons

*Scanning QR codes requires a web-enabled smart device with a QR code reader app and a camera.